TOM HOLLOWAY is an award-winning Tasmanian playwright. His work has been staged extensively both in Australia and internationally. His plays include: *Beyond the Neck* (2007, winner AWGIE Award for Best Stage Play); *And No More Shall We Part* (winner 2010 AWGIE Award for Best Stage Play, 2010 Louis Esson Prize for Drama in the Victorian Premier's Literary Awards); *Don't Say the Words* (2008, shortlisted for the 2009 NSW Premier's Play Award, Young Vic/Theatre 503 Season Award); *Red Sky Morning* (2007, winner R. E. Ross Trust Development Award, Green Room Award Best New Writing for the Australian Stage); *Love Me Tender* (2010); Fatherland (2011 Premiere The Gate Theatre London, invited to Munich Volksbuhne's Yung Radikal Festival, Munich) and *Faces Look Ugly* (2011 Premiere Århus Teater Denmark, winner the Max Afford Fellowship).

Tom is currently working on commissions for Melbourne Theatre Company, Bell Shakespeare and Tasmania Performs. He is a Contributing Artist to Gambling (Soho Writers' Theatre, London, 2010) and was resident writer with Soho Writers' Theatre in 2010. He has written the libretto for an adaptation of the film *The Secret Life of Words* that will be produced by the Bavarian State Opera at the 2011 Munich Opera Festival. He is collaborating with Matthew Lutton on a staging of Schubert's *Winterreise*.

From left: Erin Dewar as G, David Whitely as M and Sarah Sutherland as W in the 2008 Red Stitch production. (Photo: Gemma Higgins-Sears)

red sky
MORNING

tom holloway

CURRENCY PRESS

SYDNEY

CURRENCY PLAYS
First published in 2011
by Currency Press Pty Ltd,
PO Box 2287, Strawberry Hills, NSW, 2012, Australia
enquiries@currency.com.au
www.currency.com.au

National Library of Australia CIP data

Author:	Holloway, Tom.
Title:	Red sky morning / Tom Holloway.
ISBN:	9780868199054 pbk.
Subjects:	Australian drama–21st century.
Dewey Number:	A822.4

Typeset by Dean Nottle for Currency Press.

Cover illustration and design by Emma Vine, Currency Press. Based on a photograph by Gemma Higgins-Sears.

Contents

Australian Government | Australia Council for the Arts

Publication of this title was assisted by the Commonwealth Government through the Australia Council, its arts funding and advisory body.

Currency Press acknowledges the Traditional Owners of the Country on which we live and work. We pay our respects to all Aboriginal and Torres Strait Islander Elders, past and present.

A NOTE ON THE LYRICS

Introduction

Writing this introduction in early 2011 is a slightly surreal experience. This is because my involvement with *Red Sky Morning* began much earlier, in 2007 to be precise. Since that time, the play has received its original production at Red Stitch Actors Theatre in Melbourne in August 2008, been remounted at the Arts Centre in Melbourne in June 2009, and travelled to five states during a national tour through Performing Lines in late 2010.

This is not a bad return for a first draft written during a frenzied forty-eight-hour lockdown while Tom Holloway was at the Royal Court in London. It was this draft that I read when I first met Tom in early 2007. The Artistic Director of Red Stitch, David Whiteley, and I had discussed the idea of a writer's residency to develop new Australian work at the company. Prior to that point, Red Stitch had made its name importing the best new international writing. We were interested in a scheme in which texts would be developed over time with a continuity of personnel: myself as dramaturg and then director of the piece, and actors who had worked on the development following it through into production. Tom had been recommended to me as a possible writer and we met at Degraves Espresso in the city. We got on wonderfully and I left with a draft of what became *Red Sky Morning*.

Most of the qualities of the eventual piece were present in this first draft: the three family members sharing their inner monologues; the twenty-four-hour time frame; the heartbreaking tragedy of miscommunication; an authentically and economically drawn country town setting; and of course the form—synchronised, overlapping monologues written in three columns. However, there were some important differences. Most significantly, the overlapping of the three voices was only loosely structured. For the vast bulk of the piece three people were simply talking at once with less attention to how the monologues overlapped.

The innovative form of *Red Sky Morning* immediately piqued my interest. I had been harbouring a curiosity about theatrical forms that reflected the way we receive information in the modern world. For me, plain vanilla naturalism did not necessarily reflect the speed with which we absorb information or the density of that information. For instance, when we watch television, news programs bombard us simultaneously with weather details, headlines in scroll bars, footage and sound, yet we have no trouble in keeping up. In other words, what interested me about *Red Sky Morning* was that it appeared to be theatre for a contemporary attention span. While conventional wisdom was that an audience couldn't follow two people talking at once, I suspected they could as long as it was sufficiently tightly controlled.

What was even more interesting about *Red Sky Morning*'s form was that it perfectly matched its content. Tom had managed to create a form that mirrored the confusion and anxiety of depression. Moreover, for a piece that explored people's inability to communicate, putting characters in the same room and making us privy to the inner monologues was a master stroke.

Over the next eighteen months, we set about our experiment to develop a play with the same cast who would perform it. Tom, myself, and David Whiteley, Sarah Sutherland and Erin Dewar, developed the piece across a series of workshops and individual meetings. To begin with, we took the play apart, working on each of the individual monologues as if they were stand-alone pieces. When Tom was satisfied with the shape of each part, he began the process (and the herculean act of formatting) of putting the pieces back together again. We would then test the precise combination of overlaps with myself and the actors. It was at this point that we came to talk more and more in musical terminology—what was an aria and what was a trio? How could you best employ cacophony? Or silence? Throughout this time the contribution of the actors was invaluable. Quite simply, the piece could not be what it is without them. Apart from needing to hear the text out loud to make sense of it, the characters were gradually forming in front of our eyes. Each actor's performance began to grow as the voice of each character grew.

As these workshops wore on, we began to think more and more about the staging of the piece. Like most great writers, Tom gave the creative team absolute licence. This was fortunate given the scale of the challenge. The literal-ness of the direct address form demanded sensitive treatment. Too much illustration of a line like 'I go to the shower' could be deadly. Letting the text do all the work (what we referred to as the 'three actors on stools' approach) could be equally stultifying of an audience's imagination. Then there was the challenge of multiple interior and exterior spaces as well as fantasy sequences. Like most great design solutions, when the answer came it was relatively simple—a three-panel by two-panel venetian blind cell where we could open and close the blinds to create different spaces. Thus 'the box' was born and the images that came to be associated with the show.

Flash forward several years and the box had made its way to Hobart. It was an unseasonably cold night in November 2010 and all of us were gathered for the final leg of the play's national tour. The cast, David, Sarah and Erin, had been on the road for twelve weeks. Myself, the set and costume designer Peter Mumford, and the lighting designer Danny Pettingill, had all flown in. The only creative absent was Kelly Ryall, the sound designer and composer. And finally there was Tom Holloway, the writer returning to his home town. As Tom was taking a well deserved bow with the cast I couldn't help thinking back to our first meeting over coffee several years earlier. A great deal had transpired in all of our lives in the time between. But one thing was for certain: our experiment of creating a work over a long period with the same artists had been a success. The Red Stitch production of the play may live again beyond November 2010. Whether it does or doesn't, it has been one of the most satisfying creative experiences of all of our careers thus far. Most of all, we look forward to seeing what other artists will make of the gift of *Red Sky Morning*. Over to you.

Sam Strong
Dramaturg and Director
February 2011

From left: Sarah Sutherland as W, David Whitely as M and Erin Dewar as G in the 2008 Red Stitch production. (Photo: Gemma Higgins-Sears)

Red Sky Morning was first produced by the Red Stitch Actors Theatre at Red Stitch Theatre, East St Kilda, Melbourne, on 29 August 2008, with the following cast:

M	David Whiteley
W	Sarah Sutherland
G	Erin Dewar

Director, Sam Strong
Designer, Peter Mumford
Lighting Designer, Danny Pettingill
Production Manager, Linda Hum

Red Sky Morning was developed in conjunction with the Red Stitch Actors Theatre.

CHARACTERS

M, mid 40s male
W, mid 40s female
G, late teens girl

PLAYWRIGHT'S NOTE

Stage directions are in italics.
Lyrics sung or spoken by characters are in italics.
Lines said simultaneously are in bold.

We see M.

He looks at his hand.

He makes a fist and opens it.

He does this again.

M: I…

Yeah.

I'm outside.

It's dark and I'm outside in the garden. In the backyard. In my backyard. The sky's… The sky's…

The sky's clear and I can see all the stars and that's good because I… I… I love? I bloody love? Yeah, I bloody love looking at the stars.

The moon's…

Wait.

The moon's real bright and because of it I can see everything. The lawn. The barbie. The clothes line. The trees.

My shed.

I…

I whistle? No. Hum.
Mumble. Yeah. I
mumble and sing but I
can't sing. Can't sing
to save. So I kind of
mumble and sing this
song I like because,
well, I'm looking over
my backyard and, well,
it's a great bloody
song.

*Give me a home among
the dum daa
With lots a la di da
A dog or two and a
barbie…*

Right.

I stand looking over
the backyard and—

But…

Wait…

Then. Then I. Then I
see…

There's something…

In the dark I can see
something. Suddenly
I can see something.
Something big.

Something…

A…

A dog.

A dog?

Is that right?

Yeah, a dog. I can see
a dog. As my eyes get
used to the light I see
this dog just sitting
there, looking at me.
It's big. Real big. I
kneel down. I kneel
down because I like
dogs. I bloody love
them. So I kneel down
and hold my hand out
a bit towards it and I
say…

Hello boy.

G'day, big fella.

> *He clicks his tongue
> a bit, inviting it over.*

Hey?

> *He clicks his tongue
> a bit, inviting it over.*

Hey, big fella?

Come on. Come on.
You want… You want

a tummy… You want
me to give you a big
old tummy rub?

Yeah, I say that
because that's. That. A
dog person. That's the
type of person I am.
Yeah?

Yeah. I look over
my yard and hum
to myself and try to
give a dog a tummy
rub because that. All
that. That is the type
of person I am. And I
think… I think what a
lovely… ahh… What a
lovely bloody moment
to have at the end of a
day. What a brilliant
little bloody moment,
you know? You, ah…
I think that and I kneel
down and call the dog
over for me to give it a
tummy rub and—

But…

But then…

Jesus.

No.

Then it…

Jesus, it growls.

It sits up and growls
at me. Growls low and
bloody fierce and I
say settle down fella
and whoa big boy but
it growls and I see
its teeth. Its spit. Its
claws. Then just like
that it. Jesus. It leaps
straight at me and I
can't move. Can't even
get my bloody legs to
move and all I can do
is crouch there and put
my arms up over my
head and the dog flies
through the air right at
me and I jam my eyes
shut and, and feel…
and my blood. I feel
blood as the dog… this
dog, this giant dog is…

This giant dog is…

But…

> *He says nothing for a*
> *long time.*

No.

But then…

No.

I look up and I can't
see any…

Where did…

*He opens and closes
his fist.*

*Give me a home among
the…*

Funny, bloody dog.

We see W.

*He says nothing for a
long time.*

*She takes a sharp
breath in.*

I go inside.

*She goes to cover her
mouth.*

I shut the back door
and head back inside
the house.

She relaxes.

I call out to my wife.

W: **I…**

Wait.

I call out to my wife
to see if she's still up
but—

Wait…

But there's no answer,
which means she's in
bed already and—

I lie on my back.

Yeah and I think… I
think how I just can't
wait to join her.

Wait.

Yeah. I lie on my back
in bed and I… I'm
kind of asleep already

I turn out the lights in
the kitchen—

and I'm a bit dreamy
and **I…**

And I turn out the
lights in the living
room—

And I…

And I'm tired and I
think of my wife in bed
and I can't wait to join
her because…

Yeah.

Because…

I…

Because I bloody love
her.

I…

I lock the front door.

I fart.

*She makes the noise
of a big, loud fart.*

*He looks for a
moment like he hears
something.*

I've…

I've been lying in bed
and feeling the fart
build up inside me and
my belly get big and

I…

I've been dying for
it to get there. Lying
there so close to farting

Still.

but **still** dying for it to
get to that point where
it will fly out and when
it does. When it does
get right down there
in my bum I hold it
in and I hold it in and
then when I can't hold

The house is dark and
still and I look over the
living room—

And kitchen, with a bit
of moonlight coming in
around the blinds and
I smile a bit because
this is…

This is my home.

This is my family's
home.

And that's good.

That's good?

Yeah, that's bloody
good.

I mean… My family
is… I'm a lucky
bloody man, yeah?

Yeah.

My wife.

I don't want to wake
her in case she's asleep
already so I try and
quietly walk down the
hall to our bedroom on,
like on my tiptoes.

it in any more I just
let it go. A big, loud
stinky—

Mmmmm.

Yes.

I lie there.

Alone. I lie there alone
and soak it up.

Then…

Oh yeah…

Wait…

Yes.

I lift the doona up.

I lift the doona up and
I let it out and—

Smell it.

I get to the door and
quietly. Real quietly
I turn the handle so it
doesn't squeak.

It stinks. It really—

I go to open the door—
and...
This is good.

And it feels great.

I go to open the door
and...

I breathe it in.

I lift the doona up a
bit and let the fart out
and take in a big breath
and it stinks... it stinks
so...

I love, I bloody love
getting into bed with
her so I open the door
ready to creep in
beside her and I open
the door and—

Oh no.

And...

Oh shit.

There's a funny smell.
I—
Oh, my...

I think my...

Oh no, my husband.
He's walked in and...
and he must be...

Oh God! No! Oh!
That stinks! What the
bloody hell is—

My...

My...

My fart really stinks
and I didn't know he
was going to walk in
just then or I would

have… I mean I never
would have… but he
must… he can't not
smell it.

No, I can't…

I roll over. I roll over
like I'm asleep and I
know he must be—

She stirs under the
doona and when she
moves the smell gets,
like another wave of it
comes and—

I hear him breathe in
and then choke a little.

Like egg. Like, I don't
know… rotten—

Yeah.

What is that?

My fart.

Oh. Well I… My wife
must have… I should
be used to it I guess. I
mean it's not like. Not
like I haven't smelt
it… or done it. It's not
like I haven't done it to
her a million…

I can feel my cheeks.
He just stands there.
**I'm red. I can feel I'm
going red.**
**I'm red. I can feel I'm
going red,** which is
stupid because he's…
I mean he's seen…
heard much worse but
why is he just standing
there?

Why?

I… for some reason I
get embarrassed, which
feels stupid because…

because… and I want
to—

I want him to—

I do want to get in. I   **I want him to get in. I**
want to climb in next   **want him to climb in**
to her and…   **next to me and…**

I should just try. Try
to wave it away for a
second and just get in
the bed and…

Fuck me.

Lie next to her.

I mean really fuck me.

I mean, not sex. I'm
not talking about sex.

Fuck me so hard.

I just mean, you
know… curl up with
her and sleep, but I'm
not talking about—

I would love it if he
just. If he jumped into
bed and grabbed me
and—

I love just curling up
with her. Real close
and warm and… I love
that.

I would love it if he
grabbed me and pulled
me over onto my back
and—

It feels good. Actually
it feels really. Like
there's no more…

Kissed me hard and
grabbed my—

Her skin's real soft and

she's always so warm.
Almost too warm and
I…

How does she make
her skin so…

**I stand here and
think about curling
up real close with her
and with my hand on
her** beautiful breast—

**As she sleeps and it
gives me comfort.
It gives me a lot of
bloody comfort.**

I'd bury my nose, you
know. I'd lie close and
put my nose right up
against her skin and—

Her skin's real soft and
warm and I think of
putting my nose right
onto her shoulder and
her hair.

And—
**You know. She.
She's like this. This**
amazing.

Really grabbed my tits
in his big hands and
kissed me hard and
told me…

I am going to fuck you.

**I lie here and think
about him grabbing
me and with his big
hands on my tits. On
my…**

**As he tells me he's
going to turn me
round and put me on
my hands** and knees
and fuck me hard
and fast and I need
it. I need it so bad
because… because…

I feel so…

Because…

**You know. He. He's
like this. This…**

No.

There's no. I mean there's no...

There's no. I mean there's no bloody time she's more beautiful than this. She's bloody glorious and. Yeah. And. Yeah.

I lay there and I breathe her in and I place my. My hand on her breast. Her soft. And I push my body. My whole body against hers and it's. It's completely. This is completely. You know? You know? This is. I mean even better than sex in some ways...

I want him to get in bed and put his hands on. To push me onto my back and put his big hands down on my tits and lean down and kiss, on the lips, kiss me hard and then turn me over and fuck me. Fuck me so...

Hard in the—

But

But I...

You know?

But I...

No.

No.

But I...

No.

No, I stand here.

But he just stands there and I feel...

Jesus.

Dumb.

She.

He.

I walk over and lift the doona and...

Sometimes I just feel
so dumb, you know?
Like everything I do
is just the most stupid
thing in the…

But I want to lie there
next to her and hold
her and… so I lift the
doona and get in bed
and I get into bed and
she has her back to
me. Yeah. And I think
I want to reach out. To
reach out and touch her
soft…

Who would want to
make love to me when
I am so—

So I lay still, and as
I lay huddled next to
her. Next to that skin.
That smell. Her skin.
As I lay there… I reach
out a little to touch her
back—

What was—

Just for a second and
I…

He touched me?

But…

He…

But she…

He touched me!

She flinches.

I flinch. I didn't even
feel him get into bed
but he's made it in
and he touches me
but I flinch because…
because I…

Yeah.

Because I wasn't
expecting—

She flinches like she
doesn't want. Like
she's asleep and she
doesn't want me to
touch her. Like…

Yes! Yes! Touch me!

So I pull away.

No!

I pull away.

No, don't!

But…

He pulls away like he's
changed his. Like he
doesn't really want to
and… and…

Because…

But.

No.

But.

No.

I.

Well, I don't want to
wake her.

*He looks at his hand.
He opens and closes
his fist again.*

*She takes a sharp
breath in. She goes
to cover her mouth.*

I sleep.

All night.

I don't move.

I lie.

I…

It's good, good enough
just to have her, yeah?
To have her there next
to me. **I…**

I don't…

I'm bloody lucky to
have her and to get to
spend each night with
her and that's… that
is…

    I sleep.

To get to spend
your whole life with
someone is…

    Uneasy.

So I think about her.

    But I sleep.

I lie there and I think
about her and…

    In—

and…   **and** out of…

I think about our life
together and…

    I think I. That I have
    these dreams of…

I think about her and—

I think about her and   **I dream about him**
me and our daughter.   **and me and our**
                    daughter.

                          We see G.
                          Her eyes close and
                          her head drops for a
                          second.

My daughter is, well,
she's bloody beautiful.

    I think.   G: **I**…

    Am I…

Bloody…

                          Umm.

I want to…   **I want to…**

                          I'm in bed.

Time goes.

Is this right?

Yeah.

Slowly.

And…

And it's, hold on…

I don't move.

Yes.

Yeah.

I sleep…

I've been sleeping all night and dreaming, you know… kind of… I think I've had these real, well, nice dreams because as I wake up I'm… I'm all… I'm hugging my pillow like it's… like I've been kissing it. And I don't want to wake up because I'm sure the dream I was just having was real, real nice and…

M *gradually closes his eyes.*

W slowly closes her eyes.

A dog or two and a…

W *opens her eyes.*

M *opens his eyes.*

What…

I sleep.

Wait. What time is it?

It's real early.

I…

Wait a sec.

I don't even…

God. Is it…

No.

No.

I can see… umm… I look out the window and I can see a bit of

Is it morning already?
Is it really…

Did I sleep through the
night?

pink sky.

A tiny little bit of pink
sky.

I can't see the sun yet
or anything like that
but I really like that
tiny bit of pink sky
because I think, umm,
about the sun coming
up somewhere else
and how it's kind of
happening right now,
which is real cool
and kind of means
it's coming here soon
and I really like that.
Like someone else is
getting the sun coming
up right now which is
cool for them and that
I'll be getting it soon
which is real cool for
me.

I get up. I get up and
go to the shower.

Yeah.

There's… hang on. I'm
in bed and I look up
and past the bedroom
door I see… was that
an elephant?

What?

Huh?

I get up and look
down the hall and, yes.
There's this elephant.
It ducks into another

room. I. I follow it
and then in the room
I see. There's a steak
on a plate and. What
is this room anyway?
I've never… Oh. I'm
dreaming.

Oh.

Oh but now I know
I'm dreaming which
means I must be pretty
close to waking up.

Oh.

Yeah.

Yeah.

I feel around the skin
on my forehead and I
find, yeah, is this right?

The elephant starts
eating the steak and
singing…

**I look in the mirror
and see my hair all
sticking up on one
side, and dribble.**

**I, umm, find a zit. A
big zit right up in my
hair and I… and I…**

**Some dry dribble on
my cheek. My skin
is puffy and with my
hair sticking up and
the dribble I look like
a bloody bunyip.**

*It's a lovely day today
And whatever you
want to do
It would be lovely to
be—
doing it with you.*

Do I?

Wait.

Hang on…

Yes. I know. I know
Mr Elephant. I'm
dreaming, but. But
don't let me—

Oh no.

I shower.

No, please. You keep
eating. That's fine.

You know, somehow
you look surprisingly
familiar. Yes. You look
just like—

Yeah.

No.

I find a big zit and—

Oh no.

I shouldn't touch it but
I—

You're going.

I know I should just
leave it alone but now
I know it's there and I
can't. I can't stop—

I see the elephant.
It looks so familiar
but then it suddenly
grabs the plate in his
trunk and runs off
and as he runs off his
big elephant bum, it
turns… I don't know.
White? Yes, I see it
turn white right in front
of me and it's right
in my face! This big
white bum is right in
my—

I wash all the crusty
dribble off.

Oh. It's the pillow. I've
opened my eyes and
it's the pillow, not—

It's like the only thing
I can feel anywhere is
this giant throbbing zit
on my forehead—

I knew that.

Going boom boom

boom and my hand, my hand moves up towards it and I'm thinking no, no don't do it.

I get dressed.

My wife rolls over.

Don't do it!

But my hand keeps moving and before I know it, before I know it I'm thinking, yeah do it! Do it! Go on, do it!

No, don't…

And I do. I reach up and find it with my finger and I, and I, and I…

No.

No.

No.

I don't want to wake up.

I squeeze it. I use my thumb and my… what's this one called?

I shut my eyes and shove my head into the pillow because I am not awake. I don't want to be a… Just a little… a bit more… please just let me have a bit more…

Pointy finger? Yeah. And I squeeze it with those two fingers and feel it, feel it, feel it explode and it's so big and I can feel the puss and stuff spurt out into my hair and I look, it's dark but I look at my fingers and I can see there's a bit of blood on them and I think, I think…

And I get my keys and—

I am asleep. I tell
myself that I am still—

Oh.

Wait.

Now the throbbing is
worse.

Yes.

I leave.

The pink sky.

Yes I am…

I love waking up early
like this and looking at
it because it makes me
feel real… I dunno.

Do I?

No.

It's like watching
TV, you know? Like
watching that pink
sky coming is just like
watching TV and I love
TV 'cause it's… it's
kind of…

Useless. It's totally…
I open my eyes. I roll
over and my husband's
not there and…

*You know we belong
together*

No.

*You and I for ever and
ever*

No.

*No matter where you
are*
You're my guiding star

Yes.

He's gone and my
hand's on his pillow.

I think about this

teacher.

My mouth is dry and
the doona is wet. Did I
try eating it? Was that
the steak…

Yeah.

Oh dear…

**I leave the front door
and walk to my ute
and I. And I** get in my
ute and as I sit there
and look around my
street… my neighbours
and things… I feel
this… I don't know… I
suddenly feel this…

**I hear something. Not
sure. A door? Do I
hear a…**

**I think about lying
here with this teacher
from school.**

I stick my head up and
look around the room.

Mr Young.

My street. My
neighbours.

I stare at him in class.
He's so strong and
smart and his eyes are
real…

Bloody.

Dreamy. Real cool and
dreamy. He could be
on TV for **sure.**

Shit.

I hear…

My…

I think about him and
me lying here together.

I tell myself it's
**nothing and drive off
down the street.**

**Yeah, that would be
sweet.**

I think I—
hear…

Here in my room.
I think about him

coming in my bedroom
window and I can't
even say—

I love. All these streets
that I've grown up…
grown up on… My
chest… like heartburn
or…

I think about him
tapping on my window
and then coming in and
I say—

What is this? What's
going on?

My dad—

My…

Bloody hell.

What if my dad…

I love getting up every
morning and driving
down here because it
reminds me…
but…

But he doesn't care if
my dad finds us and—

These streets that I
love in this place that I
love, but—

He comes over to my
bed and I say—

But this ache in my…
I've got this strong
ache in my chest and **it
really does hurt like
there is something…
I don't know…
some kind of weight
sitting right here
in my chest. Like
there's something
in there making it
hard to breathe and**

**But what about
school? What about
school, because he's
my teacher and what
will they say? But he
says he doesn't care
about that because he
loves me with all his
heart and that he's**

I feel… like I want to… I blink and hold my chest and look out over the streets and…

come to take me away and we have to go right now because the cops are onto him for some terrible crime that he didn't commit, and, and, and…

I hear his ute driving off down the road. It always wakes me up, hearing that. This morning it makes me think about last night and…

I hold my chest and I start to feel… I don't know… this thing. This low thing aching through my chest and it's a beautiful morning and everything but…

But I can't help feel like things are… like it is…

Jesus.

No. This is… no. No. No…

From the very first moment I saw you

I never felt such emotion

The streets and the homes and knowing the face and name of every person that lives in them and I love that. I really…
I really love this place but my chest feels so heavy and low and

I guess I should get up.

like there is this thing. This—

Thing and I hold my chest a bit and rub it and don't think about it and try not to think about it and—

No.

Yeah.

But... Jesus... I can't... so I pull over. I can't concentrate and I pull over and the morning sun is in my eyes and I feel like I might... I can't believe this but I feel like I might cry. Really. Suddenly I feel like I could really just start crying as I sit here in my ute and that is... that is not... cry? No. No. That isn't me. That's not what I... but my chest and looking around and this feeling growing through me like it might... like I might... Jesus, like I might just bloody...

The day.

I should get up.

No.

I should get up. I've got things to...

Yeah.

Soapies. They're my fave. They are just **so... so...**

Real and stuff. Life in them is so...

I mean that's what it should be like I reckon. That's what real lives should really be like. For sure.

Yeah. They're just so real, you know?

But.

But no… No… No…

I'm…

I'm a bloody fool.

No. It's nothing. I
tell myself… I look
around. I don't think
anyone has seen me.

You bloody fool.

No.

The sky's all pink.

The shop. I'm fine so I
drive to the shop. I can
breathe. I'm not going
to… so I drive to the
shop.

Yeah.

Yeah, I drive down the
main street and park.

But.

I…

Yeah.

Wake up.

But.

I'm…

Yeah.

Yeah.

I look at the clock.
It's about six. Dad
would've driven off to
work already—

Before me and Mum…
before we get up, like
he does every morning.

Maybe my dream was
about Mr…

He's so hot.

I figure I might as well
get up and I've got
to do everything real
quiet 'cause Mum's

still in bed.

Mum?

I hear someone
walking around.

I get up and get
dressed into my school
uniform.
**My jumper and pants
and...**

I go into the bakery a
couple of doors down
and pick up a coffee
and a bun for my
breakfast.

It's my daughter—

Nah.

My daughter leaving
for school and I...

My jumper and skirt.
Yeah.

I do it so much it's
sitting there waiting
**for me. I put my
money down and take
it and call out... call
out...**

**I get my bag and get
dressed and sneak
down the hall so I
don't wake Mum.**

I hear her walk down
the hall.

Cheers Dave.

I eat a bowl of rice
bubbles and I know I
shouldn't, that they're
for little kids—

Yeah.

But I still like them so
I have some and I leave
them out for Mum with
a bowl and a spoon and
the milk. So I leave
them out for her to
have when she gets up

I call out cheers Dave because he's a good bloke. Bloody good bloke. And I go and open the shop.

Yeah.

I go and open the shop.

The locks. The alarm. The lights. The till.

I stand at the counter.

I look over the shop.

I love this shop.

I stand and I look over

I hear the door shut.

I hear her walk off.

I'm alone. In the house, all...

I'm alone so I get out of bed and I walk around the house.

I open some blinds to let the light in. Just a little bit. Those two never open the blinds and I stand in the nude and open them a little.

I go to...

To the cupboard.

I get a beer out.

I put it in the freezer.

---

and I go.
I tiptoe out of the house and go to school.

The sun's up and everything.

Everything really kind of glows, you know?

I walk alone. I walk along the street and—

Oh.

But I'm no loner. It's not like I'm some kind of loner. It's too early for most kids to be going to school yet so I just walk on my own.

I...

Yeah.

the shop and I drink
my coffee and eat my
bun.

While I walk along
I practise my model
walk and clench my
bum.

I sit down next to the
freezer and I wait.

I look at the counter
**and I see the marks
my hands have worn
in the wood.**

**You gotta put your
foot down in the
middle in front of** you
each time so your hips
move.

I'm nude. The light
comes in through the
gaps in the blinds and
I sit and wait for my
beer and I'm nude
and—

Smooth.

That's how they do
it. It looks real nice I
reckon. Real…

Nice.

**The freezer vibrates
a little bit and I put
my face next to it and
it tickles my skin so I
have to rub it off.**

**Feminine and because
I've got my skirt on I
walk along and think
about being on some
catwalk with flashes** going off all over the
place and the whole
crowd, hundreds,
thousands of people
watching me and
saying I look real hot.
Real pretty and hot
and… and like I am the
most… the…

I look over my shop.   **I look at my body.**

But then I look at my
stupid short legs and
my stupid short arms
and my stupid fat bum
and I wish, I mean I
really wish I could
look just a bit…

I look at the grocery
section.

My boobs are so, so
saggy. Look at them.
Floppety flop.

Yeah.

I look at the hardware
section.

My arse.

I look at the recreation
section up the back.

I walk.

My shop…   **My big,** cold, round
curdled cream of an…

The zit on my head is
still sore and I reckon
I'll get another pick at
it later.

And my bikini line
is… well it doesn't
exist. I mean since
when do I wear bikinis
anyway? How can
I even call it… it's
like there's just this
giant bush of fur that's
crawling down my legs
and up. Even up my
belly. Since when does
my pubic hair grow
up my belly? It's like
if I let it, and the way

I'm going I probably
will, it won't stop. I
can see the headline
now. Woman found
suffocated by her own
pubic—

Then I'm at school.
In the yard. I get there
early and—

I think…

I…

It's cold but real bright.
I sit on a…

I'm looking at my
body and it all looks
so…

Yeah.

Funny.

I sit on a bench against
a brick…

I should really… I
should do something
about…

People come.

It's wet. The wall. The
bench.

The little bell at the
door tinkles.

I put my bag between
my legs.

Always the same
people.

There's no teachers yet
even. Just a couple of
cleaners.

Yeah.   **Yes.**

I think about going and
waiting for Mr, you
know for—

Wait.

Mr Young.

Regulars.

People I know. People
I've always known.

Yeah. I think about
going and waiting in
his carpark for him
to get here. He drives
this, this real cool car.
Don't know what it is
but…

Yes.

I stand and look over
at them all. These
brilliant people. And
I…

But it's real cool and
I think about him
arriving and seeing
him get out and shut
the door and he's…
I know he's old and
stuff but still there's
something… I don't
know. Like strong.
Like his arms look real
strong and his hair—

I don't care that he
doesn't have much—

Wait…

My chest…

Hair left and
sometimes I like to
think of him getting
to school and seeing
me and coming over
and grabbing me in
his arms and telling
me that he… that he's
going to look after me
and… and…

Yeah. Have a chat
with them because. It
might sound funny,
but…

Yes I fall asleep for a
moment. My wrinkly
old face feels funny
from the freezer. The

Yeah.

I bloody love—

tiles are cold on my
giant bottom and legs.

Yes.

And my hand is… is
in my pubic… like for
warmth. Like my pubic
hair is so thick that
while I slept my hand
went down there for
warmth. Jesus, Mary
and—

I sit on the bench.

Mornin' love.

It's real quiet and I
sit and it's quiet and I
close my eyes a bit.

I…

I…

It's a fresh one isn't
it? Yeah, she'll heat up
though.

It's a lovely day to—

*She closes her eyes
for a moment.*

Mornin' darl'.

Don't.

What… what was?

I wake. Shake myself
awake a bit. I open—

Do I? Yes. Yes, of
course I do…

Did I sleep just then?

I hear something and…

I open the freezer and
the beer is still a bit
warm but I drink it
anyway.

Yeah, she's a bit chilly
this morning isn't she?!

Meant to heat up later though.

Breathe…

G'day mate. It sure was a struggle to get outta bed this morning, wasn't it?!

Give me a home among the...

With lots a plum...

I have a chat.

It's great to get to say

I'm naked in the kitchen.

I sit in the nude on the kitchen floor and my face tingles like it's all numb.

Wait.

Yes.

And my body looks so… so. When did I let this happen?

I wonder that and I drink my warm beer.

It flows down my throat and then hits my belly. The taste is strong but I'm used to it.

I should…

I should do something.

Teachers arriving.

Mr…?

Kids come. They play.

Guys play footy. Girls sit around.

My friends all come and sit around with me.

Julie, she's probably my best—

My friends and me, we sit around and talk about cool stuff and—

g'day, you know?

I just sit there and
every now and then
I look over at the
staffroom to see if—

I finish the beer.

And I see Julie looking
over at me as I look at
the staffroom and—

I stand. I put the can in
the bin.

It's bloody great so I
have a chat and then—

I say to Julie, when
she's looking this one
time at me and I don't
want her to, I say—

Don't.

Your hair looks real
beautiful this morning
Jules and she says
thanks and tells me
about her shampoo and
stuff and stops looking
at me like that. We all
sit around and laugh
and hang out and that's
kind of it until the bell
goes.

And…

I go to the bedroom
and get dressed. I don't
shower. I don't put on
make-up.

No.

Normally I do.

What is this thing?

Normally I love a bit
of make-up, but not…
not today…

We all go to class and we sit…

Jesus.

Yeah.

I look at the bed and think about last night and… I make it and **then I** get dressed. His clothes are in a pile on the ground so I pick them up and I take them to the laundry and put them in the machine and…

Then I—

Suddenly everything. I mean it all seems…

Hang on, do I?

We sit around in class like we sit around outside. We pass notes and stuff.

No. Stuff it. No I don't pick them up.

I'm…

I move away from the counter.

I leave his clothes in a pile on the ground.

I'm not sure but I think I move away from the counter. I…

We.

I should do something. I'm going to do something for me. Yeah. I'm going to jog! I'm going to go jogging!

I walk through my shop.

I walk through the
groceries and smile at
Ange.

**I've known Ange
since I was a kid.
She's quiet and all
but a good soul I
reckon. And her
daughter goes to
school with my
daughter and…**

I ask her, how's Julie I
ask and she says good
and I keep walking. I
feel the thing again.
Like I could just cry
any second and I walk
through the hardware
and check with
James—

Wait…

Wait…

I get dressed. I don't
shower. I don't put on
any make-up. I leave
his clothes in a pile on
the ground.

I don't get my
daughter's clothes.

I don't. I'm not going
to. I just don't care. I
stop and I put on my
sneakers because I am
going to jog!

I get a beer.

Just one before…

I wanna…

I.

**We sit around and
I kind of take notes
because it's Mr
Young's class and
he's so… so… but my
friends just sit around
so I don't take too
many.**

But then…

Do I?

Yeah.

Yeah it's James. It's
James who's Ange's
husband. Yeah.

I take it to the kitchen
table and drink it, just
to get me ready for a
big, old jog.

Then when we're all
reading some book…

I check with James if
I can help him at all
and I liked James as a
kid but I never really
see him anymore and
I think, that's bad. I
should do something
about that and I hold
my chest.

The warm metal of the
can against my lips.

We've got to read
this chapter of some
dumb book, well Mr
Young—

I should definitely do
something…

**I should invite them
round for a barbie or**
something and I feel
bad that I haven't done
it already. I mean our
daughters are… are
friends and…

He comes up behind
**me and bends down
and I go all…**

The dull fizz of the
beer running down my
throat and into my—

I feel all…

Belly.

I rub my…

I walk past Ange. I walk past James and I head to the back of my shop and it's growing in me and people are seeing me like this and at the back of my shop, in the recreation area there's William. He's the town doctor and he. Wait. Yeah. He delivered my daughter.

William is a keen **fisherman and he likes coming in and looking at the flies I have for sale. I walk down past him and I—**

Is this—

I ask him. Is this right?

I sip at it. Small, quick sips. **Drinking down the whole can like that as I sit in a bit of that morning daze.**

I leave. I'm really going to… I take some beers and leave the house to go jogging.

I leave the house and I walk. I leave the house and I go for a walk to warm up. Then I will run.

The sun is…

I dunno…

But he leans down and he says to me do you like the book? And I look at him, I just look at him and smile and nod and he's looking at me like…

I know he's looking at me like he's telling me what he wants, you know? I can see it in his eyes and his smile so I…

My heart is real… I feel all… and I think maybe he's going to. Like he's leaning down because he's leaving me a note or something to say…

Bright.

Yeah…

Right, to say…

So he kneels there with his hand on my desk and I think about there being a note in this hand that he drops as he leaves and I…

I feel so…

I squint.

Yeah…

I open it and it says. It says he loves me and he knows I feel the same and that he wants to. To…

If they're biting.

He wants to take me away and he tells me to meet him at lunch at his car and that we're gonna go. Just get in his car and go and never come back and he has some place in the city where we can… where we will be together and I sit there in the car with him and he drives and I move over and put my head on his shoulder and my hand on his leg and close my eyes and know that. That what we are doing is… is real… like love. Like real love with the sun setting and the open

I walk down the street but not towards the shops. Not to drop in and see my… say a quick hello to my husband and get a bit of a kiss and… Instead I turn right and walk. There is a park and I feel like jogging in the park. I see William the doctor walking to work. No. Walking from his work to the shops. He waves at me and I wave at him. I hide the beers in my big, it's handy to have a big handbag when beer is what you want to drink and…

I walk down to the
recreation area and,

Yeah, ask him if
they're biting and he
says.

He says not as much
as he would like and
he chuckles. He asks
about my daughter. I
tell him my daughter
is beautiful and that
she sure didn't get
that from my side of
the bloody family and
now she's a terrible
teen which she did get
from my side of the
bloody family and he
chuckles. He… No.
Yeah. He chuckles
and I. I feel… Do I…
I… I… Yeah. I pop
into the back room
where I keep a couple
of guns and things
that farmers buy
from me occasionally.
I keep them back
there locked up.
I pop into the back
room and I…

I reach for a gun.

I get my key and open
the special safe and
reach for a hunting
gun from the shelf

I.

No.

No I don't.

But why not?

Yes.

Yes I…

I wave.

Yes.

I wave back at him.
Yes.

Why wouldn't I wave?

He's a nice old… and
I'm just out for a
jog, which is a good
thing. It's a really
good thing so I do. So
I wave and he walks
on and so do I and I
walk to the park.

There are big gum
trees. A few banksia.
Some play equipment.
And the church we

road and nothing but
each other and, and,
and…
No matter where you
are
You're my guiding star
And from the very first
moment I saw you
I never felt such
emotion
I'm walking on air
Just to know
Just to know
You are there
You are there
Hold me in your arms
Don't let me go
I want to stay forever

I wish that would…
I really wish…
If that could just… if
it could…
But then I think about
my legs and my bum
and know Mr Young
would never… But…
I go to classes. I take
some notes. I don't
talk to my friends. I
don't pay much.

I just daydream
about…
Different class.
Different class,

and I am still chatting
with William through
the door and he
chuckles at a joke I
make and I load the
gun, and he chuckles
and I walk back out
and—

I shoot him in the
heart. Yeah. I shoot
him in the heart and.
And blood. There's this
spray of the blood. I
walk through it. I walk
through the blood and
down to James and I
shoot him in the heart
too. He doesn't. He
just stands there and I
shoot him in the heart
and there's more…
In the… it's on my
clothes. On my skin. I
shoot him in the heart
and his blood hits me
and then I…

Then I.

Then I go to Ange.

I go to Ange.

I go to Ange and I. I.

I go to Angela and I—

I tell her. I ask her. I
ask her to tell my wife.

got married in. The
park we had our
reception in. I'm
going to jog. Right
now. Right… This is
it. This is…… I sit. I
go and sit. I go and sit
on a bench.

same…
I mean…
But…
And I feel…
As the classes go, I
feel…
Is this right?
I feel a bit…

To tell my daughter. I
ask her to tell my wife
and to tell my daughter
I'm sorry and then I. I
ask her to tell them I'm
sorry and then I put
the gun in my mouth
and I pull the trigger. I
ask her to tell my wife
and tell my daughter
I'm sorry and I put the
gun in my mouth and
I reach for the trigger
and I push the trigger.

And I—

I—

Jesus!

No! No! No I!

That's stupid! Sick!
That's sick! That's…
That's bloody… I
don't! I wouldn't! I
would never! I would
never do that!

Then at break.

I…

Then at break. At
lunch.

At lunch my friend,
Julie, she says…

Is it? Is that? Is it? Do
I…

Yeah.

Open a beer. Take a
drink and sit it back

I'm sitting down with
my friends and I'm

down in my bag.

not listening to them
because I'm feeling…

No.

The sun.

I dunno…

I…

Weird.

Yes.

It's a lovely day today

**And then Julie she
looks at me and I
don't really know
what we've been
talking about but
then suddenly she
says—**

No.

*And whatever you've
got to…*
*It would be lovely to
be…*
*And if there's
something that must
be done*
And it can only be…

**How's your mum?
She says did you have
to hold her hair away
from her face this**
morning?

No.

In a bitchy imitation:

Except for saying…

Did you have to hold
your mum's hair away
from her face this
morning?

I stand there at the
counter.

She says this and I
mean. Everyone kind
of knows. I mean I take
Mum's beer for my
friends.

**In the gum trees
I hear a couple of
magpies and I sit and
close my eyes and**

**They know that she.
And I always joke
around about it with
them but I'm feeing**

listen to the magpies
and their sound...

No, I stand there at
the counter.

weird and Julie, she's
my best, but now
she says this and I.
I don't know, I. For
some reason I...

I hit her.

She says...

And.

I hit her.

I punch her in the face.
I punch her in the face
real hard and she falls
back on the ground
and I jump on her
and punch her again
and scream at her to
mind her own... I say
this... Mind your own
fucking business and
I keep whacking her
with my hands and I
grab her hair, her long
ugly hair and pull it
and I yell at her to
mind your own fucking
business and I spit in
her face. How dare
you. How dare you say
that about my mum!
Bitch! Stupid bitch!
Slut! Fucking slut! And
my other friends try
pulling me off and it
takes four of them and
again I spit at her and

I'm so…

Like fuck it! Fuck it
all! It's fucked! It's
totally fucked. And I
wanna, I just wanna…
I mean I really fucking
just wanna…

**I stand at the
counter and I look
over my shop and
I have a chat with
my customers and**
for a moment. Just a
moment I think I might
move…

**The trees and the sun
and the magpies and
it's a lovely day and
I see red and I listen
and I drink my—**

That I might move
and…

No.

I don't think I… No, I
don't.

Wait.

They're. My friends.
They're just standing
there. Like they're.
Standing. Like,
shocked at. At me
and… and…

Yes.

And my friends…

Yes.

They stand there like
they're shocked at…

I drink my warm beer
and look at it and…

They stand all shocked
and they're looking at
me and Julie's on the
ground and she says…

I feel. I feel this can't

go on.

Why don't you fuck off
to Mr Young?

Yes. I sit and see red
through my shut eyes
with my beer in my
hand and I think what
am I doing? Look at
me, I mean really look
at me! What on Earth
am I doing?

I...

I look at her.

I look at all of them
and they're staring
at me and it's like
everything here...

Wait...

Like today everything
here in my life really...

I cry.

I mean...

I sit there.

Like really fucking
sucks.

And I cry—

Everything really
fucking sucks.

James asks me
what the tune is I'm
whistling and I tell
him... I say I don't
know actually and
he says really and I
say yes I don't know
and he says that he
has always wondered
what that tune was
that I kind of whistle
and hum when he's in

I get this anger and
I'm frustrated and
I'm sad and it's all
because he nearly
touched me but
didn't because a... a
because everything
is so fucking... I
mean... The things
I have done for him
and he can't even
touch me?! He can't

here.

Give me a home
among the gum trees
With lots of plum trees
A dog or two and a
barbecue
Some dum da down
the back
Some da di dum da
And an old rocking
chair
Give me a dum di…
With lots of la…
A dog or…
And a barbie
Some something down
the side
Some dum di da da—

He looks at his hand
again. He clenches
his fist and releases
it.

even fucking.

I stand up and I go to
the church. I walk to
the front of the church.
I look at it.

Sandstone. Old. I
think about walking
out the entrance in
my white dress with
him looking so, so
handsome in his suit.

But…

I feel this horrible
thing hanging over
us and I just can't
take it. I just really
can't… I take a beer.
A full one. I take the
beer can and I scream
out I CAN'T TAKE
IT ANYMORE and I
throw the can at the
church. I throw it as
hard as I can at the
stained-glass window
over the door and I see
it smash the window. I
see it clear as day and
I don't care. I don't.
I take my other cans.
I throw them too. It
smashes more and
more and I scream
out damn you God!
Where the hell are
you?! You're a joke!

I go.

I walk away.

I walk away.

You're a big stinking
useless joke and I hate
this church and I hate
my husband and I hate
all this shit! It feels
good. It feels so... like
finally I can, I can, I
can...

He says nothing for a long time.

She says nothing for a long time.

She says nothing for a long time.

No.

I walk out of school.
No-one stops me.

No.

I don't break the
window. I don't yell.

**I get a can out of
my bag and skull it.
Stand there at the
church and skull a
whole can and I am
angry, yes, and I
throw it but it doesn't
break** the window.
I don't even reach
the big stained glass,
because I can't. Can't
throw at all and I really
**try but it just bounces
off near the bottom
of the wall and back
onto the ground in
front of me and I take
the empties from my
bag and do the same
with them. Throw**

**I stand at the gate.
I'm dizzy. Everything
comes... My face
turns red and I... for
a second I... I dunno,
I can't walk and I...
like I might fall over
or...**

**I'm shaking real bad
and my hand hurts
where I punched her
and I can't believe
I... I'm a psycho!
I'm a stupid fucking.
Everyone knows. How
could I be so stupid?**

them at the church one by one and it feels good but also... The way they just bounce off...
The cans just bounce off and sit there on the ground in front of me...

God.

What am I doing here? I mean...

Has it really come to...

God.

I can't believe...

Shit.

I...

I feel... I don't know. Like I'm not here. As I sit here in the park I really feel myself...

As if they didn't. As if they didn't know about my parents and about Mr... that I like stupid, ugly, old Mr Young because I'm a stupid dumb...

I run home.

I stand outside.

I've got the stitch.

I stand outside, but I don't. I don't wanna go in because what if Mum's...

Stupid Julie.

Man, if Mum's in there and—

I open the gate real quiet. I walk down the path real... I go to the window. The blinds are only open a bit but I try to look in to see if she's there.

I don't know but I… like I'm floating. Like as I'm sitting here I'm actually floating off to…

I don't see her. I get my key and, real quiet, open the door.

Please don't let Mum…

I can't say really. But it is like I'm floating off above myself looking down at me sitting here in front of the church and I don't… Like there's nothing the same between the me floating up here and the me sitting down there. Like we're not even the same person.

I go in and shut the door. It's hard being quiet 'cause I've run home and I'm breathing hard and stuff but I try and shut the door real softly. She's not in the living room. The rice bubbles and bowl and stuff are still sitting there. The milk's gone off. I chuck it out. I tiptoe down the hall and slowly sneak a look in her bedroom but—

What is happening?

I look around.

She's not there either. I walk around the house but she's not anywhere, which is weird but I'm just glad she's not here. I sit down in front of the TV and curl my legs up and I sit here for hours. Just sit here and watch TV.

The day goes. People come. People go.

Somehow I've been

here all day and I
notice the light has
changed and suddenly
I'm back down inside
myself and I look at…
I see…

Ange?

Jesus.

She stands there above
me and sees me sitting
on the ground. She
says—

Small talk.

She says hello and I
say hello. She asks
how my daughter is
and I say—

Shit.

Good thanks and she
asks how my husband
is and I say—

Pathetic.

Great. She asks me
what I'm doing and I
say—

What am I doing?   **What am I doing?**

Jogging. She says it's
a lovely day for it. I
say—

No.   **No.**

It sure is and she
stands there so I. I get
up and. And leave the
cans like they're…
they're not mine. Not
anything to do with…
and I jog. I can barely

stand. I mean my head
is… all the beer and…
she looks at me and
smiles blankly so I just
jog off. Back home. I
try and…

I can't think.

I go home. Tonight,
things will… Tonight I
will… I must… I must.

Then after a couple
of hours. I hear Mum.
Hear her walking down
the path and she comes
inside and when she
walks in I…

I walk home. My
daughter's inside.

I can smell it on her
and I don't even look
at her. I ignore her.

I say to her.

Yeah.

Do I?

Yeah.

Yes. I see her and I say
to her… Steak's for
dinner.

I lock up the shop.

**She's watching TV
and all I say is steak's
for dinner and she
says nothing.**

**I watch TV and she
says something about
dinner but I can tell
she's… the smell's**
real… so I just ignore
her.

Yes.

It's the end of the day
and—
I fill a bag with some
stuff and lock up the

She says nothing.

I.

shop and turn the
lights off and pull
the blinds down and
lock up the shop and
I drive home. I get in
my ute and I drive.

It's parked out the
front of the shop and
I get in it and I drive
home.

As I drive the cicadas
and crickets. They are
everywhere. Louder
than the car. Like a
radio off bloody station
and they're there all
the time.
For the whole drive
and I can feel this
ache in my head
growing from them,
dull at first but as I
listen to them more
and more and then...

I don't tell her what
I've done.

I don't tell her about
my sneakers or the
park or anything. I just
say...

I start cooking and she
says nothing.

Then I. I reckon I
want to...

I reckon I want to tell
her.

I want to tell her
about Julie because,
like maybe it will... I
don't know, but...

Because it's just her
and me in the house,
so... so maybe if I
tell her about Julie
and what she said
then something will.
Like. Yeah. Because
I want it to change. I
really need it to change
and maybe if I say
something to her now
that it's just her and
me, even if she has
been... so I do. I do
say something. I look
over at her and I turn
down the TV and I
look over at her and I

My head pounds.

Huh?

say… I say…

Mum?

But…

Then with the cicadas and my head and this whole bloody thing, this whole bloody day, then when I pull up at home I can barely think from the ache in my head.

My daughter mumbles something and I ask her what she said, but…

But when she looks at me, well I see the rice bubbles still on the bench like she hasn't even seen them still and I just go back to the TV.

I sit for a moment in the car before opening the door to get out and when I do—

I get some steaks out and some vegies. Some carrots and some spuds and—

I stay quiet.

I…

Damn it.

The noise.

It's like it's even louder and I stumble out of the car and—

I…

I just want this to be over with! I just want to be able to feel like a normal bloody human being!

I just…

My mum…

But as I stumble out of the ute I can't take the noise and I trip over on the drive and I'm down on the ground and my hands are burning and—	**But...**	**But...**
my leg feels, and the noise just goes on and on in my head like it... I don't know... Like it... **like** it won't give up until I...	**My...**	**I...**
	Like...	**Like...**
No. No I won't... I can't. Can't let it... No! This can't...	**No.**	**No.**
	Then.	
		Then.
I get up. I want to see my family so I get up.		
		Then.
I can hear them inside and I want to see them so I get up and brush myself off and go into the house—		
And try and ignore the dog and the sting on my hands and the pain in my leg and what happened at work and inside is my wife and my daughter and I look at them both.	**I start cooking and before too long my husband comes in and I feel this need to, this urge to go and...**	**Then Dad comes home and now we're all here and...**
	My husband.	
My wife.		
		My dad.
My daughter.		

I want to go and hold…

Now there's no point in trying anything.

To go and hold…

This all…

And they make me feel so…

I turn up the TV.

Hold him and. I don't know. Plead. And plead and…

I go up to my wife.

I can't believe this but I want to throw myself at his legs and plead with him and I want him to pick me up and hold me and tell me… tell me everything is…

I go up and kiss her.

I want us to make it better. I want… so when he comes in and kisses me on the head. When he comes and kisses me on the head, then I say to him… I say…

I go up and I kiss her on the forehead and smell her… Smell her hair and it smells like love. No. No that's—

kisses me on the head. When he comes and kisses me on the head, then I say to him… I say…

I don't look at Dad and I don't look at Mum and I say nothing and I watch TV.

Yeah. Yeah it smells like…

I say…

I don't.

And I go over to my, to my daughter.

I don't move when he kisses me on the head.

I go over and I kiss her
on the forehead and
smell her hair and it…

I just watch TV.

Yeah. It smells like
love too. Not the same
kind, but…

Darling.

Darling, please…

But still love.

And it feels so good
to come home to this
and I suddenly get
this wave of, this huge
wave of… that this is
what it is all…

But.

What was…

Darling, please…

My wife says
something to me and…

I want to throw myself
at him and tell him
everything and for him
to tell me everything
will be better. When he
walks in I say to him,
I say,
**Darling? I say,
Darling, please…**

**Mum and Dad and
Julie and Mr Young**
and the sun and sitting
on the bench and being
in class and thinking
about Mr Young and
everything…

*M looks at his hand.
He looks at if for a
long time.*

No. He looks at me,
confused, like I've
broken his line of
thought and…

I kiss them both on

I

the head but they,
each time they just…
almost… like they're
trying to ignore it.   **Try.**
Like it makes them,
bloody makes them
uncomfortable and…
Jesus. They act like   **Jesus.**
I'm, almost like I'm   **I'm…**
annoying them or
something and I get
distracted when I
think **my** wife says   **My.**   **My…**
something to me—

I smile and I say
nothing. Beer. I want.
No. I do—
But she just smiles,   **But…**
but blankly, like she
smiles blankly and I
feel my hands burn and
the pain in my leg and
neither of them, neither
of them even look up.
They don't even…

I really want a beer.

I sit down. I sit down
and I can't help but
have this feeling. This
terrible… Like. Like.
Like there is no need
for me to be here. Like
I'm bringing nothing
to what is happening
here. I give nothing.
That's exactly… But
it's my house and my
family and I think.
I think. I think how.
How did this happen?

How did this happen
to me?

        He just sits there.

I look at my wife.

        I cook some carrots.

I look at my daughter.

        I want a.

They don't look at me.

        I really want a…

They don't look.

        Mum asks Dad if he
wants a beer and she
says it like it's her first
and like it's okay so I
say…

They don't talk to me.

        It's dinner time so I
think why not so I get
a beer and I offer one
to—

My wife.   **My husband** but he
gestures no and my
daughter asks for one—

        Give me one.

Her skin.

        And I ignore her but I
get a beer.

        I say that. Like maybe
it will make her
think… think about…
but she just ignores me.

        I ignore her.

I open the beer   **Dad says nothing**
and pour it into a   **to Mum. She says**
glass and I pour too   **nothing to him. We**
quickly and…   **don't talk. We…**
Yes I pour too quickly
and it gets a big head
and I drink the bit that

doesn't fit in the glass
and as it goes down my
throat I feel—
the cold spread through
my body.

My daughter. Sitting.
Watching TV. My
wife, cooking and
drinking a beer.
She in her world.
My daughter in her
world. Me in—

I put the can in
the bin and get the
frying pan and heat it
up hot ready for the
steaks.
You must use a hot
pan for steaks. I
drink my beer. The
head dies down. The
amber colour glows. I
drink my beer. I put
butter on the pan—

Yeah. Really. We
don't talk. We don't.
Is this? Is this right?
Is this what families
are like? I dunno. I
feel like something's
wrong and it's like
everything feels wrong.

I stand. I get up.

The beer.

Then Dad.

The butter sizzling.

Then Dad, I know what
he's going to do.

The cool spread
through my—

I must.

I sit.

I must.

I sit.

The smell of the butter.

He gets that look like
he gets and I know he's
about to…

The tingle down my
back.

Should I?

I stand up and my heart
is raging, but this feels,

it feels like what I have
to…

The heat of the pan.

Should I? I think, yeah.

The buzz in my head.

I think yeah I think I
should get up and stop
him walking outside
and that this is the time
to…

I drop a steak in and it
screams.

Nah…

I walk out.

My husband.

I get up and I walk out
the front door and the
crickets and cicadas
are still there. Still
making that noise. That
horrible…

It screams in my
head over and over
like some machine.
Some bloody machine
boring right down
into me and my heart
is raging and I walk
to the ute and I get
my bag of stuff and I
go to my shed.

I watch him get up
like he is going to
head out to his shed
and I think I say
something. I think for
just a flash. Yes I…

Dad, he gets up and
just stands there for
a minute like he does
every time before he
heads out the back to
his…

Mum drinks a beer.

No.

I sit.

I stumble down the
side of my house with
the bag to the shed.
To my shed and I put
the bag on the bench
and I look at it and I
move to the window

I drink my beer. Then
I drop the steak in the
pan. Then I barely
notice him get up and

Mum fries a steak. I
turn up the TV.

and look up and see
the light of the TV
and I go back to the
bag and I open it.
And I get out the gun.
And I look at the gun.
I get out the bullets
and I look at the gun
and the bullets I think
how many times.
How many times do
I have to stand here
and ask myself this?
Why can I not bloody
shake this? Why
does it always bloody
follow me? My whole
bloody. Why can't I?

I open the gun.

I open the gun and I
place in the gun one
bullet.

I open the gun and I
place in the gun one
bullet.

I look at the gun.

I—

walk out to the car. I
cook the steak for a
minute and then I flip
it over and it screams
again. I see the light
go on in his shed. I
don't move the steak.
You must not flip it
more than once and
you must not move
it. You want to sear
it. I drink my beer. I
take the steak out and
put the next one in. I
put the vegies out and
flip the second steak
over and it screams
too. Things must end
tonight but…

But after the steaks are
cooked…

I call to my husband.

I.

Yes I call to my
husband but he doesn't
come so I send my
daughter to get him.

She drinks her beer
and Dad walks out
and I don't care.
I like TV. I like
watching TV. I
like soapies. I like
'Neighbours' and I
like 'Home and Away'
because they make
me feel real… I mean
real… I wish I could
just… I don't care
what's going on. I
don't give a shit.

Mum. Then Mum says
to me. She tells me.
I'm watching 'Home

**Why do I always get
these pins and needles
in my hand? Why
does it always. Why
does it—**

*He smacks the hand
with pins and needles
into the other. He
does this loud and
hard and over and
over.*

**My thoughts. The
noise. The gun. This
feeling. This feeling.**

I don't want to but I.
But—
I.

Shit.

Fuck.

Fuck.

I don't want to but I

*She takes a sharp
breath in, goes to
cover her mouth.*

**The park. The beer.
The church. That
feeling. That feeling.**

Tonight I will talk!
Tonight I will reach
out! Tonight I will—

Shit.

Shit.

Fuck.

I get another beer.

and Away' but Mum
tells me to go and get
Dad. That dinner is
ready and I have to go
and get Dad—
**And I want to tell
her to go and stick
her dinner and Dad
and everything up
her...** where the sun
doesn't... but...

She closes her eyes.

Her head drops.

Her head drops.

She wakes.

I do.

I go outside. I walk out
the door.

I walk down.

I walk down the path
down the side of the
house.

pick up the gun.

I walk down the side of the house and—

I put in the gun one bullet.

Head down past his ute and down the path because he must be—

I kneel down on the ground.

I guess he must be in the shed.

I turn the gun around **and—**

And so I head down there and see the light on inside so I…

Shit. And. Shit. Shit.

I head to the shed.

I turn it around and I'm going to. I'm really going to do it and I think yeah. Yeah. Yeah. Yeah. And I kneel there and I put the gun in my mouth and close my eyes and then. Then. Then…

I shouldn't but I get another beer and I, from the fridge and I skull it. I skull it right there and then…

Dad? Hey Dad?

I hear a sound. A little…

I open the door.

I open my eyes.

I open the door and…

My.

My daughter.

She's.

She's standing in the
door and—

She's looking.

She's.

I want to.

I want to say.

**I want her to come
over and take the gun
and I want to collapse
in her arms and into
her lap and cry. And
cry. And wail. I want
to be held in my
daughter's arms. I
want her to hold me.
I want her to take the
gun and let me** cry
and wail and hold me.

I see Dad.

He has a gun.

Pointing…

The barrel in his…

He looks at me.

I.

I want to. I want to go
and…

**I look him in the eyes
and I'm scared and I
see in his eyes. In my
dad's eyes. I see this
thing. This. This. This.
I dunno what it's. I've
never seen it before.
I've never. This look
like he's… Like he.
Like he's trying to.
Like he really…**

I want her to tell me it
will be all…

                                        I…

I want to yell at her,
please?

                                        No.

Please help me?

                                        No.

Please help me from
all this? Can't you just
please—

                                        Shit.

Can you help me? Can
you get rid of this?
Of this horrible…Can
you?!

                                        I…

She stands there.

                                        I want.

She looks.

                                        I don't want.

She sees the gun.

                                        He.

She sees me.

Mum.

She.

This whole.

She.

I can't.

She.

I can't do…

She walks away.

I leave the shed.

She walks away.

I walk away.

She walks away from.

I turn around and walk
out of the shed and
leave him there and…

She goes back inside.

Then my…

I go in the back door.

Then.

She.

My daughter.

I stand at the back door
in the kitchen.

She looks…

I shut the back door.
My mum…

I don't know but…

The taste of metal.

She looks…

My daughter. She's
standing there at the
back door.

I don't know but I see
her and suddenly I…

The oil on my lips.

She starts to cry.

My arm stretched.

I cry. I'm scared. I'm
so scared.

I don't…

My thumb on the.

Mum.

On the trigger…

I don't understand.

I…

                                          I should.

She…   **She's** standing there
at the door and I see a
tear. A little tear and…

                                            I need to…

And there is…

                                            Oh God, I'm so scared
and I need to tell her
before he… before
he… but I can't. I can't
get anything out and…

There's a tear.

                                            No!

She stands.

                                            No!

She cries.

I tell her.

                                            She closes her eyes.
She cannot hold off
the need to close her
eyes and her head
drops and it looks
as if she is about to
faint.

I want to tell her.

I want to tell her this
will end but…

She cries and she
shakes her head and
then…

> *She breathes in*
> *sharply and goes to*
> *cover her mouth.*

The gun, it slips out
of my hands onto the
floor.

I sit.

There is. There is
nothing I…

She knows. She saw.

> M *says nothing for a*
> *long time. He does*
> *not find an answer.*

I stand up.

I walk to the…

I go into the…

My daughter, she's
there and…

My wife looks…

They…

I sit. I sit at the dinner
table.

They look at me.

I sit…

My wife, she picks up
a plate and puts it. Puts
it in front of me. They
sit down.

We sit there with our.
Our…

The smell of steak.

We…

We start…

We start to…

We start…

THE END

www.ingramcontent.com/pod-product-compliance
Lightning Source LLC
Chambersburg PA
CBHW041932090426
42744CB00017B/2025